ISBN 0 7188 2129 7

Set reference: 1/2a/4

First published in Great Britain 1975

D1390008

Titles in this series:

Made and Printed in England by Wightman & Company Ltd.,
Cranmer Road, London, SW9 6EJ

Major and minor scales

Compiled by Alfred Hossack

System by Mentor Textbooks

LUTTERWORTH PRESS
Luke House   Farnham Road
Guildford   Surrey

Training Notes

This book has been compiled to help those wanting to learn about the structure of music, whether they are studying for examinations or not. Since it is self-correcting it is ideally suited to those working on their own. For this reason it may also recommend itself to teachers who wish to provide students with remedial work, revision courses or pre-course study material.

Three-way text
This text may be used in three different ways, according to the need of the reader or the judgement of the teacher or training officer.
1.   General study or selective study. Readers work through the whole text, or through selected sections of the text (see Contents page).
2:   Revision. Readers use the text as a self-tester, working through the exercises at the foot of each page and studying the instructional matter only when they have been stopped or branched as the result of an error.
3.   Reference. Readers may refer to any particular subject aspect by looking up the index at the back of the book.

Testing procedures
Testing is continuous throughout the book. No reader can complete the text until he (or she) has answered every question correctly.

Proficiency grading at a glance
The Mentor system does away with the need for marking or work correction. But it is recommended that readers jot down, on a work record sheet, each *attempted* three-figure solution they produce. Then they—or their instructor—can award a grading at a glance on the basis of the number of attempts required to complete the course. A suggested marking scheme is laid out on the final working page. A sample Work Record Sheet is available to those ordering this text in quantity.

Immediate diagnosis of difficulties
A Master Sheet is also available to those ordering this text in quantity. This sheet gives the correct solutions and branch solutions, in working sequence, as well as the subject matter. By relating the Master Sheet to any individual Work Record Sheet, areas of difficulty can be detected immediately.

Contents.

How to use this book

1. Start on the following page. Like all working pages in this book, it has a three-figure number at the top. All page numbers are in ascending order (100, 200, 300, etc.) but many page numbers are missing.

2. Read what the page has to say. Then look at the questions.

3. Choose ONE of the three possible answers against Question A—and note the special number at the end of the answer you choose. Then do the same with Question B. Then do the same with Question C.

4. You now have a three-figure number. Look for a page with this number in the book.

5. If there is a page with the number you have found, resume work on that page. If there is no page with your number, then do the exercise again until you do find a page with your number.

If you jot down on a sheet of paper each three-figure solution you obtain—right or wrong—you will be able to award yourself performance marks at the end. This will also ensure that you do not lose your place as you work through the book.

The word 'scale' means 'ladder'. A scale in music is a ladder of notes. The rungs of the ladder are the notes themselves, each note being a little higher in pitch than the note below it. This difference in pitch is called *interval*.

Whole tones and half tones

Note intervals are seen most clearly on the keyboard of a piano. This keyboard, as we all know, is a pattern of white notes and black notes. Every black note separates two white notes—even though it is not so long as the white notes it separates.

The *interval* between any note and the note next to it is called a *half tone* (or semitone). So the interval between a white note and the black note next to it is a half tone. And the interval between two white notes *with no black note between them* is also called a half tone.

When any two notes are separated by one other note—white or black—then the interval between them is a *whole tone*.

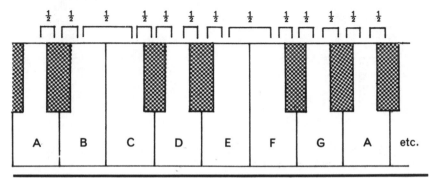

Choose the correct answer in each of the following.

A. What is the interval between the white note C and the white note D?

One half tone	**1**
One whole tone	**4**
Two whole tones	**7**

B. What is the interval between the white note D and the white note E?

One half tone	**2**
Two whole tones	**5**
One whole tone	**8**

C. What is the interval between the white note E and the white note F?

One whole tone	**3**
Two whole tones	**6**
One half tone	**9**

You have failed to grasp an important point.

You chose the wrong answer to questions A and B in the last exercise—and you made exactly the same mistake in each of them. Look at the white notes C and D again and you will see that there is a black note between them. Look at the white notes D and E again and you will see that there is a black note between them. Now let's go through the last lesson again.

Whole tones and half tones

Note intervals are seen most clearly on the keyboard of a piano. This keyboard, as we all know, is a pattern of white notes and black notes. Every black note separates two white notes—even though it is not so long as the white notes it separates.

The *interval* between any note and the note next to it is called a *half tone* (or semitone). So the interval between a white note and the black note next to it is a half tone. And the interval between two white notes *with no black note between them* is also called a half tone.

When any two notes are separated by one other note—white or black—then the interval between them is a *whole tone.*

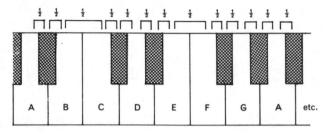

Now tackle the repeat exercise below.

Choose the correct answer in each of the following.

A. What is the interval between the white note C and the white note D?

One half tone	**1**
One whole tone	**4**
Two whole tones	**7**

B. What is the interval between the white note D and the white note E?

One half tone	**2**
Two whole tones	**5**
One whole tone	**8**

C. What is the interval between the white note E and the white note F?

One whole tone	**3**
Two whole tones	**6**
One half tone	**9**

We have seen that we can obtain the major scale pattern of intervals (1 1 $\frac{1}{2}$ 1 1 1 $\frac{1}{2}$) by playing all the white (natural) notes from any C to the C above it. But, if we want to start on any other note, we must use *accidentals*. These accidentals can be sharps (page 937). They can also be *flats*. Let's try a scale from F.

Flats in the major scale

If we play all the white (natural) notes from any F to the F above it, we get this pattern:

1 1 1 $\frac{1}{2}$ 1 1 $\frac{1}{2}$

The problems here are the third and fourth intervals. From A to B should be a half tone—but it is a whole tone. From B to C should be a whole tone—but it is a half tone.

We can adjust this by lowering B to B flat—this gives us a half tone between A and B flat and, at the same time, increases the interval between B and C to a whole tone:

1 1 $\frac{1}{2}$ 1 1 1 $\frac{1}{2}$

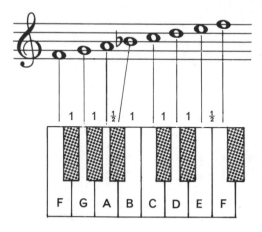

When we lower a natural note by a $\frac{1}{2}$ tone (e.g. from B to B flat) we have *flattened* it.

Choose the correct answer in each of these.

A.	What is the required pattern of tone intervals in any major scale?	1 1 1 $\frac{1}{2}$ 1 1 $\frac{1}{2}$	**2**
		1 1 $\frac{1}{2}$ 1 1 1 $\frac{1}{2}$	**5**
		1 1 1 1 1 1 1	**8**
B.	We can obtain this pattern by playing all the white (natural) notes from ...	any F to the F above it	**1**
		any G to the G above it	**4**
		any C to the C above it	**7**
C.	If we want to play a major scale from F to the F above it, what must we do?	flatten B	**3**
		flatten F	**6**
		sharpen B	**9**

So notes can be *natural*, *sharp* or *flat* and, when a composer writes down music, he has to make a distinction between them. Obviously he does not want to keep writing 'sharp', 'flat', etc. Instead he uses symbols to indicate these words.

Accidentals

Here are the symbols. When they occur during a passage of music they are called *accidentals*:

♮ = natural   ♯ = sharp   ♭ = flat

Since the *natural* notes are the ones most commonly used, it is assumed that a note is *natural* unless otherwise indicated. So A always means A♮. B always means B♮. And so on. Here is the piano keyboard again, this time naming the black notes as well as the white notes. Study it carefully.

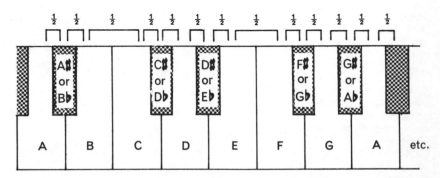

Sharp, flat and natural symbols are called 'accidentals'.

		natural **1**
A.	The symbol ♯ means ...	flat **8**
		sharp **9**
		sharp **2**
B.	The symbol ♭ means ...	natural **6**
		flat **7**
		natural **3**
C.	The symbol ♮ means ...	sharp **4**
		flat **5**

We now know how to build *upwards* from one major scale to the next. We use the second four notes of one scale as the first four notes of the new scale—and we sharpen the seventh note of this new scale.

Building major scales upwards

We have seen how to build upwards from C Major to G Major. Now let's build upwards from G Major.

The *second* four notes of the G Major scale are D E F♯ G. We now use these as the *first* four notes of the new scale—and we sharpen the seventh note of this new scale.

We can see that the first note (tonic) of this new scale is D. So this new scale is in the key of D Major.

Observe that this new scale of D Major is four notes higher than the G Major scale from which it was formed.

Observe too that this new scale has *one more sharp* than the G Major scale.

What is the next scale upwards from D Major? How many sharps will it have?

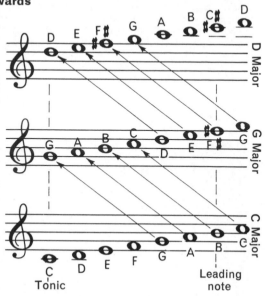

Choose the correct answer in each of these.

A.	What is the next scale upwards from D Major?	A Major	**4**
		E Major	**6**
		D Major	**8**
B.	How many notes higher than D Major will this new scale be?	One note higher	**1**
		Four notes higher	**2**
		Eight notes higher	**3**
C.	How many sharps will this new scale have?	Seven sharps	**5**
		Three sharps	**7**
		Four sharps	**9**

You chose the wrong answer to all three questions in the last exercise—
and you made exactly the same mistake in each of them. Here is the last lesson
again. Read it carefully this time.

Building major scales downwards

We have seen how to build downwards from C Major to F Major. Now let's build downwards from F Major.

The *first* four notes of the F Major scale are F G A B♭. We now use these as the *second* four notes of the new scale—and we flatten the fourth note of this new scale.

Observe that the fourth note of the F Major scale (B♭) has now become the *eighth note* (tonic) of the new scale.

Since the eighth note is B♭, the *first* note of the new scale (which is also tonic) must also be B♭.

So the key of the new scale is B♭—not B as one might have supposed.

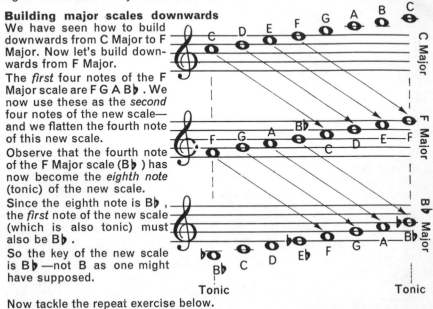

Now tackle the repeat exercise below.

Choose the correct answer in each of these.

A. What will be the *eighth* note of the scale below the B♭ Major scale?

E natural	**2**
E sharp	**6**
E flat	**7**

B. What will be the *first* note of the scale below the B♭ Major scale?

E natural	**3**
E sharp	**4**
E flat	**5**

C. What will be the key of this new scale?

E♭ Major	**1**
E Major	**8**
E♯ Major	**9**

Correct. Now read on.

We now know how to build *downwards* from one major scale to the next. We use the first four notes of one scale as the second four notes of the new scale —and we flatten the fourth note of this new scale.

Building major scales downwards
We have seen how to build downwards from C Major to F Major. Now let's build downwards from F Major.

The *first* four notes of the F Major scale are F G A B♭. We now use these as the *second* four notes of the new scale— and we flatten the fourth note of this new scale.

Observe that the fourth note of the F Major scale (B♭) has now become the *eighth note* (tonic) of the new scale.

Since the eighth note is B♭, the *first* note of the new scale (which is also tonic) must also be B♭.

So the key of the new scale is B♭—not B as one might have supposed.

Choose the correct answer in each of these.

A.	What will be the *eighth* note of the scale below the B♭ Major scale?	E natural	**2**
		E sharp	**6**
		E flat	**7**

B.	What will be the *first* note of the scale below the B♭ Major scale?	E natural	**3**
		E sharp	**4**
		E flat	**5**

C.	What will be the key of this new scale?	E♭ Major	**1**
		E Major	**8**
		E♯ Major	**9**

You have failed to grasp an important point.

You chose the wrong answer to questions B and C in the last exercise. You are getting confused between the two minor scales.

The *harmonic* minor scale has an 'augmented second'—a leap of 1½ tones—between the sixth and seventh notes. So here is its pattern:

1 ½ 1 1 ½ 1½ ½

The *melodic* minor scale is designed to do away with the augmented second. Its sixth note is sharpened. This reduces the interval between the sixth and seventh notes to a whole tone. At the same time it increases the interval between the fifth and sixth notes to a whole tone. So here is its pattern:

1 ½ 1 1 1 1 ½

Now tackle the repeat exercise below.

The melodic minor scale does not have an 'augmented second'.

A.	The interval pattern of the *major* scale is ...	1 1 ½ 1 1 1 ½	**3**
		1 ½ 1 1 ½ 1½ ½	**4**
		1 ½ 1 1 1 1 ½	**5**
B.	The interval pattern of the *harmonic minor* scale is ...	1 ½ 1 1 1 1 ½	**1**
		1 1 ½ 1 1 1 ½	**8**
		1 ½ 1 1 ½ 1½ ½	**9**
C.	The interval pattern of the *melodic* minor scale is ...	1 ½ 1 1 1 1 ½	**2**
		1 ½ 1 1 ½ 1½ ½	**6**
		1 1 ½ 1 1 1 ½	**7**

The purpose of the key signature is to do away with *accidentals*—to do away with sharp signs and flat signs in front of individual notes along the stave.

In fact, when a *major* scale carries a key signature, it has no accidentals at all. This is because all major scales are built on the *natural* major scale (C Major) which has no sharps or flats.

But, when a *minor* scale carries a key signature, it *still* has one or more accidentals. This is because all minor scales are built not on the natural minor scale (A Minor) but on an *adjusted* natural scale. The harmonic minor scales (page 675) are built on A Minor with one sharp. The melodic minor scales (pages 854 and 392) are built on A Minor with two sharps and two naturals.

Accidentals in the minor scales

As the minor scales are built *upwards* from the adjusted A Minor scale or *downwards* from the adjusted A Minor scale, the accidentals sometimes change.

When a sharp is itself sharpened (raised half a tone) it becomes a *double sharp* (x). When a sharp is flattened (lowered half a tone) it becomes a *natural* (♮).

The *naturals* in the descending melodic minor scale (page 392) are also affected. When a natural is flattened (lowered half a tone) it becomes a *flat*. When a natural is sharpened (raised half a tone) it becomes a *sharp*.

It is these complications that make the minor scales more difficult to master than the major scales. And it is these complications that are favoured by examiners. So study the minor scales at the back of this book very carefully. And make sure you know the accidentals by heart.

Despite key-signatures, minor scales have accidentals.

A.	When we raise a sharp by half a tone, we get . . .	a sharp	**5**
		a flat	**7**
		a double sharp	**9**
B.	When we raise a flat by half a tone, we get . . .	a sharp	**4**
		a natural	**6**
		a flat	**8**
C.	When we lower a sharp by half a tone, we get . . .	a sharp	**1**
		a natural	**2**
		a flat	**3**

We have just seen that a five-line stave can show only eleven different pitches of note. This is not enough to cover all the note-pitches from the bass (low) range to the treble (high) range. So different staves are needed for different ranges.

We can tell the range of any stave by looking at the symbol that begins it. The symbol—known as a *clef*—also tells us which notes are which. This is very important because the positions of the notes vary from stave to stave.

The treble clef
The treble range is indicated by the *treble clef*. This is also called the *G clef* since its pivotal part falls on the line where G should appear.

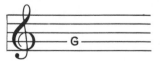

The bass clef
The bass range is indicated by the *bass clef*. This is also called the *F clef* since its two dots straddle the line where F should appear.

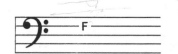

The alto clef
The alto range comes between the treble and bass ranges. It is indicated by the *alto clef*. This is also called the C clef since its centre part straddles the line where C should appear.

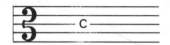

Name the notes below in the right order.

A.

A B C D E F G	1
F G A B C D E	4
G A B C D E F	7

B.

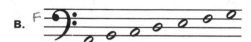

G A B C D E F	3
F G A B C D E	6
A B C D E F G	9

C.

F G A B C D E	2
∨ G A B C D E F	5
A B C D E F G	8

So, to avoid the harmonic minor scale's 'augmented second', the *melodic* minor scale has its sixth note sharpened as well as its seventh note.

The melodic minor scale (ascending and descending)

A descending scale is normally the reverse of an ascending scale. So one would expect the descending melodic minor scale to have its sixth and seventh notes sharpened. But composers in the past found that it was melodically smoother if the sixth and seventh notes were *flattened* as the scale came down. Like this:

6th 7th   7th 6th

Observe that the symbols before the sixth and seventh notes of the *descending* scale are *naturals*. When a note is flattened, it is lowered by a *half* tone. And, if we lower a sharp by a half tone, we get a natural.

So, in the descending scale of the A Melodic Minor (shown above) and in several other descending melodic minor scales, the flattened notes are indicated by *natural* signs. But this does not happen in *all* the descending melodic minor scales. The exceptions—and the reasons for these exceptions—are covered at the back of this book under 'Melodic Minor Scales'.

Choose the correct answer in each of these.

A.	Which two notes of the *ascending* melodic minor scale are sharpened?	6th and 7th notes	**5**
		7th and 8th notes	**7**
		5th and 6th notes	**9**
B.	Which two notes of the *descending* melodic minor scale are flattened?	6th and 5th notes	**1**
		8th and 7th notes	**2**
		7th and 6th notes	**3**
C.	Which accidental is used to indicate each of these flattened notes in the A Minor scale?	The ♯ sign	**4**
		The ♭ sign	**6**
		The ♮ sign	**8**

Building *upwards* from the scale of C Major, we can form seven major scales in all. Here they are below. Study them carefully and see how each new scale gains an extra sharp until eventually we reach the scale of C♯ Major in which every note is sharpened.

Each scale is shown here in two halves. This will help you to see how the second half of one scale forms the first half of the scale above it.

Major scales with sharps

C♯	D♯	E♯	F♯	G♯	A♯	B♯	C♯	C♯ Major	7 sharps
F♯	G♯	A♯	B	C♯	D♯	E♯	F♯	F♯ "	6 "
B	C♯	D♯	E	F♯	G♯	A♯	B	B "	5 "
E	F♯	G♯	A	B	C♯	D♯	E	E "	4 "
A	B	C♯	D	E	F♯	G♯	A	A "	3 "
D	E	F♯	G	A	B	C♯	D	D "	2 "
G	A	B	C	D	E	F♯	G	G "	1 "
C	E	D	F	G	A	B	C		

We have stated above that the scale of F♯ Major has 6 sharps, although it contains seven sharp signs. This is because both the first note and the last note are the *tonic*. So both these sharps count as one. The same rule applies to the scale of C♯ Major.

Once a note is sharpened, it stays sharpened in the later scales.

A.	In which major scale does D♯ appear as a leading (seventh) note?	B Major scale	`2`
		E Major scale	`5`
		D Major scale	`8`
B.	In which *other* scales does D♯ appear?	In all scales below E Major	`3`
		In all scales above E Major	`6`
		In all scales except C Major	`9`
C.	In which scales does D♯ *not* appear?	In C Major only	`1`
		In all scales above E Major	`4`
		In all scales below E Major	`7`

You chose the wrong answer to question C in the last exercise. Look at the white notes E and F again and you will see that they are *not* separated by any other note, black or white. Now let's go through the last lesson again.

Whole tones and half tones

Note intervals are seen most clearly on the keyboard of a piano. This keyboard, as we all know, is a pattern of white notes and black notes. Every black note separates two white notes—even though it is not so long as the white notes it separates.

The *interval* between any note and the note next to it is called a *half tone* (or semitone). So the interval between a white note and the black note next to it is a half tone. And the interval between two white notes *with no black note between them* is also called a half tone.

When any two notes are separated by one other note—white or black—then the interval between them is a *whole tone*.

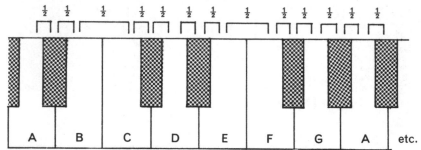

Now tackle the repeat exercise below.

Choose the correct answer in each of the following.

A. What is the interval between the white note C and the white note D?

One half tone　■1

One whole tone　■4

Two whole tones　■7

B. What is the interval between the white note D and the white note E?

One half tone　■2

Two whole tones　■5

One whole tone　■8

C. What is the interval between the white note E and the white note F?

One whole tone　■3

Two whole tones　■6

One half tone　■9

So each note of a scale is a little higher in pitch than the note below it.

Sharp, Flat and Natural

The most commonly used notes on a piano keyboard are the white notes. These are the 'natural' notes. So the white note A is A *natural*. The white note B is B *natural*. The white note C is C *natural*. And so on.

When a note is a *half tone above a natural note*, we call it *sharp*. So the black note to the right of A natural is A sharp. And C—the white note immediately to the right of B—can be called B sharp as well as C natural.

When a note is a *half tone below a natural note*, we call it *flat*. So the black note to the left of B natural is B flat (or A sharp). And B—the white note immediately to the left of C—can be called C flat as well as B natural.

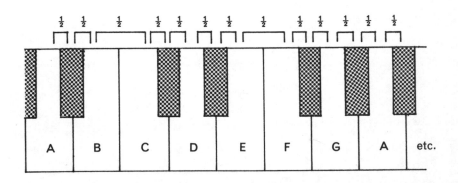

Choose the correct answer in each of the following.

	C sharp or D flat	**1**
A. What is the black note between C natural and D natural?	C sharp or D sharp	**5**
	C flat or D sharp	**6**

	F sharp	**2**
B. How else can we describe E natural?	D sharp	**4**
	F flat	**9**

	E flat	**3**
C. How else can we describe F natural?	E sharp	**7**
	G flat	**8**

There is simply no room on a five-line stave to allow separate positions for the black notes. So C sharp takes the same position as C natural. E flat takes the same position as E natural. And so on.

So how can we distinguish a sharp or a flat from a natural note on the stave? We do it by using *accidentals* (already covered on page 197).

Accidentals and the stave

There are three points to note about accidentals on the stave. First, the accidental always goes *in front of* the note to which it relates (♯♩ and ♭♩). Second, a note without an accidental is always a *natural* note. Third, it is usual to write the black notes as *sharps* when the pitch is *rising* and to write them as *flats* when the pitch is falling. The examples below should make this clear.

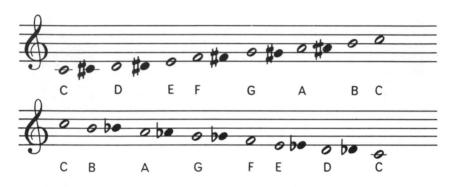

The accidental always goes in front of its note.

A.	What note is this?	B natural	**1**
		G natural	**5**
		A natural	**6**
B.	Name these notes in order	G natural and G sharp	**3**
		B natural and B sharp	**7**
		G sharp and G natural	**8**
C.	Name these notes in order	G natural and G flat	**2**
		G flat and G natural	**4**
		B natural and B flat	**9**

If we play all the white (natural) notes from any C to the C above it, we have played a *major* scale. This tells us two things about the major scale straight-away. First, it contains eight notes. Second, it begins and ends on the same note *letter*: C D E F G A B C.

The natural major scale

But the most important thing to observe about the major scale is its pattern of whole tones and half tones. The interval between C and D is a whole tone. So is the interval between D and E. But the interval between E and F is only a *half* tone (see page 100).

Between F and G we have another whole tone. The interval between G and A is a whole tone. So is the interval between A and B. But the final interval be-tween B and C is another *half* tone.

So here is the pattern of tone intervals:

1 1 ½ 1 1 1 ½

No scale can be called *major* unless it follows this pattern of tone intervals.

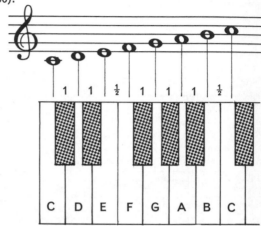

Choose the correct answer in each of these.

A.	How many notes are there in a major scale?	six notes	**1**
		seven notes	**8**
		eight notes	**9**

B.	How many intervals— whole tone or half tone —are there between these notes?	seven intervals	**3**
		six intervals	**4**
		eight intervals	**5**

C.	What is the pattern of these intervals?	1 1 ½ 1 1 1	**2**
		1 1 1 1 1 1 1	**6**
		1 1 ½ 1 1 1 ½	**7**

When a major and minor scale have the same tonic or key-note, they are known as *tonic major* and *tonic minor*. For example, the A Minor scale is the tonic minor of the A Major scale—and the A Major is the tonic major of the A Minor.

Converting major scales into minor scales

What is the difference between a major scale and a minor scale? Each has a different pattern of tone intervals. So, if we want to convert a major scale into its tonic minor scale, we must *change* the interval pattern.

Here is the interval pattern of the *major* scale:

1 1 ½ 1 1 1 ½

Here is the interval pattern of the *harmonic minor* scale:

1 ½ 1 1 ½ 1½ ½

If we lower the 3rd and 6th notes of the major scale by a half tone, we get its tonic minor (harmonic).

Here we see how the A Major is converted into the A Harmonic Minor. It

happens that the 3rd and 6th notes of the A Major are both *sharps*. So, when they are flattened, they become *natural* again. The natural signs have been put in here simply to show what has happened.

Choose the correct answer in each of these.

A.	The tonic minor of the C♯ Major scale is . . .	C Minor	**3**
		C♯ Minor	**6**
		C♭ Major	**9**
B.	To turn a tonic major scale into a tonic minor scale (harmonic), we have to flatten the . . .	3rd note only	**2**
		6th note only	**5**
		3rd note and 6th note	**8**
C.	What note do we get when we flatten a sharp?	a 'natural'	**1**
		a 'sharp'	**4**
		a 'flat'	**7**

So far we have seen how to build scales upwards from the scale of C Major. Now let us compare the F Major scale (page 196) with the C Major scale (page 532).

From C Major to F Major
In what way is the F Major scale similar to the C Major scale? The *second* four notes of the F Major (C D E F) are the same as the *first* four notes of the C Major.

In what way is the F Major scale different from the C Major scale? The *fourth note* (sub-dominant) of the F Major scale is *flattened*.

We can now see how to build the F Major scale from the C Major scale. We simply use the *first* four notes of the C Major as the *second* four notes of the new scale—and we flatten the fourth note of this new scale.

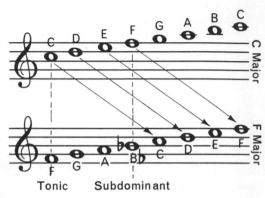

Tonic   Subdominant

Observe that we are building *downwards*—the first note (tonic) of F Major is four notes below the first note of C Major.

The first half of one major scale forms the second half of the next.

A.	What new scale do we get if we build downward from the C Major scale?	F Major	**2**
		B Major	**4**
		D Major	**9**
B.	How many notes lower is this new scale?	Three notes	**3**
		One note	**7**
		Four notes	**8**
C.	Which note of the new scale must be flattened?	The note F	**1**
		The note E	**5**
		The note B	**6**

You have failed to grasp an important point.

You chose the wrong answer to all three questions in the last exercise—and you made exactly the same mistake in each of them. You are confusing *relative* major and minor with *tonic* major and minor.

A *tonic* minor scale is a scale that has the same *key note* as its tonic major. For example, the tonic minor of the G Major scale is G Minor.

But a *relative* minor scale is a scale that has the same *key signature* as its relative major. And, as we have just seen, the sixth note of any major scale provides the first note of its relative minor scale. For example, the sixth note of the G Major scale is E (G A B C D *E*). So E Minor is the relative minor of the G Major scale.

Now tackle the repeat exercise below.

Choose the correct answer in each of these.

A.	What is the relative minor of the C♯ Major scale?	A♯ Minor	**3**
		E Minor	**4**
		C♯ Minor	**5**

B.	What is the relative minor of the D Major scale?	B Minor	**2**
		F Minor	**6**
		D Minor	**7**

C.	What is the relative minor of the C Major scale?	C Minor	**1**
		A Minor	**8**
		E Minor	**9**

Each note, or *degree*, of a scale has its own name. For example, the first degree of a scale—whether the scale starts on A, B, C, D, E, F or G—is always called the *tonic*. The second degree is always called the *supertonic*. And so on.

The degrees of the scale

Here you can see the names of the degrees of the scale from the first note to the eighth. All of them should be learned by heart. Two of them —the *tonic* and the *leading note*—need special mention here.

The *tonic* is the first and the last note of the scale. It is also called the *key-note* because it gives us the key of the scale. A major scale beginning and ending on C is said to be in the 'key' of C Major. A major scale beginning and ending on G is said to be in the 'key' of G Major.

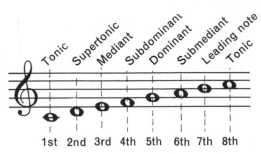

1st 2nd 3rd 4th 5th 6th 7th 8th

The *leading note* is the seventh degree of the scale. It is called a *leading* note because it 'leads' us on to the final note (tonic) of the scale. It does this because it is a *half* tone below the final note. Try playing any major scale. If you stop on the leading note, you will find you are left with a sense of incompleteness. It is only when you move on to the eighth note that you feel the scale has been finished.

Each degree of the scale has its own name.

		Dominant	**2**
A.	What is the first note of a scale called?	Leading note	**4**
		Tonic	**9**

		Subdominant	**1**
B.	What is the last note of a scale called?	Leading note	**5**
		Tonic	**6**

		C Major	**3**
C.	The tonic of a major scale is A. What is the key of the scale?	B Major	**7**
		A Major	**8**

You have failed to grasp an important point.

You chose the wrong answer to questions B and C in the last exercise—
and you made exactly the same mistake in each of them. In each case you
forgot that the accidental comes *in front of* the note to which it relates
(e.g. ♯♩ and ♭♩) when that note appears on the stave.

The only time the accidental comes after its note is when we refer to that note
by its alphabetical letter (e.g. A♯ , B♭ etc).

Now tackle the repeat exercise below.

The accidental always goes in front of its note.

A. What note is this?

B natural	**1**
G natural	**5**
A natural	**6**

B. Name these notes in order

G natural and G sharp	**3**
B natural and B sharp	**7**
G sharp and G natural	**8**

C. Name these notes in order

G natural and G flat	**2**
G flat and G natural	**4**
B natural and B flat	**9**

You chose the wrong answer to questions B and C in the last exercise—and you made exactly the same mistake in each of them. In each case you ignored the *key signature* after the clef sign. There are fifteen major keys in which a composer can write. And only one of these keys—C Major—carries no key signature. So, if you wish to read music in any of the other fourteen major keys, you *must* look at the key signature first.

The key signature is a 'once-and-for-all' instruction. If a sharp sign appears in a particular position after the clef, it means that *every* note in that position must be sharpened—unless otherwise indicated. And, if a flat sign appears in a particular position after the clef, it means that *every* note in that position must be flattened—unless otherwise indicated.

Here again are the two examples we used in the last lesson:

 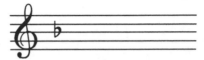

Here we have a sharp sign in the F position at the beginning of a piece of music. This means that *every* F must be sharpened.

Here we have a flat sign in the B position at the beginning of a piece of music. This means that *every* B must be flattened.

Now tackle the repeat exercise below.

The key signature makes music simpler to write and read.

	Name these three notes			
A.		B♭	D♭	F♭	**3**
		B	D	F	**6**
		B♯	D♯	F♯	**9**

	Name these three notes			
B.		B	D	F	**1**
		B♯	D♯	F♯	**4**
		B	D	F♯	**7**

	Name these three notes			
C.		B	D	F	**2**
		B♭	D	F	**5**
		B♭	D♭	F♭	**8**

So much for the major scale whose pattern of tone intervals (page 532) is 1 1 ½ 1 1 1 ½. Now let us look at the *minor* scale.

The harmonic minor scale

If we play all the white (natural) notes from any A to the A above it, we get a 1 ½ 1 1 ½ 1 1 pattern of tone intervals. This is very close to the pattern of a minor scale—indeed it is sometimes called the *natural minor scale*.

But the pattern of this natural minor scale is not satisfactory. It is not satisfactory because the last interval—the interval between the *leading note* and the last note—is a whole tone.

But, as we have seen on page 573, the *leading note* should be only a *half* tone below the last note of the scale.

So, to reduce this interval to a *half* tone, we *sharpen the leading note* of the scale. This gives us the *harmonic minor scale*:

1 ½ 1 1 ½ 1½ ½

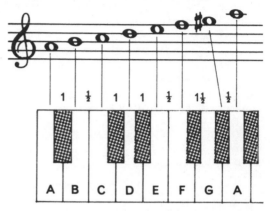

In sharpening the seventh (leading) note, we make a 1½ tone interval between the sixth and seventh notes. This is called an *augmented second*.

Choose the correct answer in each of these

A. What is the interval pattern in a *major* scale?

1 ½ 1 1 ½ 1 1	**3**
1 ½ 1 1 ½ 1½ ½	**7**
1 1 ½ 1 1 1 ½	**8**

B. What is the interval pattern in a *harmonic minor* scale?

1 ½ 1 1 ½ 1 1	**1**
1 ½ 1 1 ½ 1½ ½	**5**
1 1 ½ 1 1 1 ½	**6**

C. The 'augmented second' of the harmonic minor scale lies between the ...

1st and 2nd notes	**2**
6th and 7th notes	**4**
7th and 8th notes	**9**

So, when we convert a major scale to its tonic minor scale, we must change some of the accidentals. As a result, a minor scale will never have the same key signature (page 893) as its tonic major scale.

Key signatures in the minor scales
Here is the rule for finding the key signature of a minor scale from its tonic major scale. Memorise it carefully.

To find the key signature of a minor scale, *either subtract three sharps* from its tonic major *or add three flats* to its tonic major. Like this:

E Major	=	4 sharps
So E Minor = 4 sharps − 3 sharps =		1 sharp
F Major	=	1 flat
So F Minor = 1 flat + 3 flats =		4 flats

Sharps are the opposite of flats. So *minus* 1 sharp = *plus* 1 flat. *Minus* 2 sharps = *plus* 2 flats. And so on:

D Major	=	2 sharps
So D Minor = 2 sharps − 3 sharps =		−1 sharp
So D Minor	=	1 flat

G Sharp Minor, D Sharp Minor and A Sharp Minor have no tonic major scales:

G Sharp Minor = 5 sharps
D Sharp Minor = 6 sharps
A Sharp Minor = 7 sharps

G# Ab
D# Eb
A# Bb

Tonic majors and tonic minors have different key signatures.

A. The key signature of the C♯ Major scale has seven sharps. How many sharps or flats will there be in the key signature of the C♯ Minor scale?

Seven sharps	3
Four sharps	7
Four flats	8

B. The key signature of the A♭ Major scale has four flats. How many sharps or flats will there be in the key signature of the A♭ Minor scale?

Seven sharps	2
Seven flats	4
One flat	9

C. The key signature of the G Major scale has one sharp. How many sharps or flats will there be in the key signature of the G Minor scale?

No sharps	1
Two flats	5
Four sharps	6

Here are the key signatures of the minor scales. Note that each scale has one more sharp or flat than the one before it:

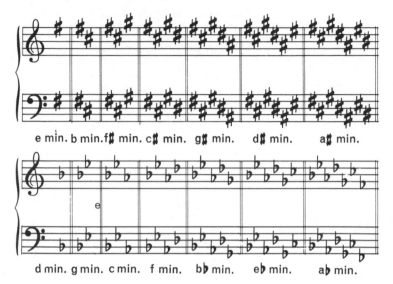

e min.　b min.　f♯ min.　c♯ min.　g♯ min.　d♯ min.　a♯ min.

d min.　g min.　c min.　f min.　b♭ min.　e♭ min.　a♭ min.

And here once again are the key signatures of the major scales. Note that, when a major scale and a minor scale have the same key signature, they have a different tonic or key note. For example, the major scale with one sharp in its key signature is in the key of G, whereas the minor scale with one sharp in its key signature is in the key of E:

G maj.　D maj.　A maj.　E maj.　B maj.　F♯ maj.　C♯ maj.

F maj.　B♭ maj.　E♭ maj.　A♭ maj.　D♭ maj.　G♭ maj.　C♭ maj.

When a major and a minor scale have the same key signature, they are said to be 'relative'. For instance, the E Minor scale (1 sharp) is the *relative minor* of the G Major scale (which also has 1 sharp). And the G Major scale (1 sharp) is the *relative major* of the E Minor scale (which also has 1 sharp). The same applies to key signatures with flats.

We sometimes need to convert a relative major key to its relative minor key. This is simple. Here is the rule.

Converting a relative major into a relative minor

The 6th note of any major scale is also the 1st note (tonic) of its relative minor scale. So by starting on the 6th note of a given major scale, we can produce the *relative minor* of that major scale.

Let us take the example of the F Major scale (1 flat). The 6th note of the F Major scale is D. So the D Minor scale—like the F Major scale—has a key signature with 1 flat:

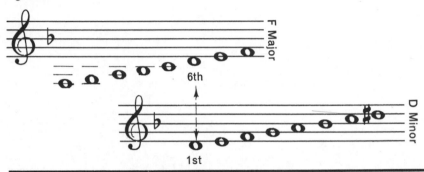

Choose the correct answer in each of these.

	A♯ Minor	**3**
A. What is the relative minor of the C♯ Major scale?	E Minor	**4**
	C♯ Minor	**5**

	B Minor	**2**
B. What is the relative minor of the D Major scale?	F Minor	**6**
	D Minor	**7**

	C Minor	**1**
C. What is the relative minor of the C Major scale?	A Minor	**8**
	E Minor	**9**

Building *downwards* from the scale of C Major, we can form seven more major scales. Here they are below. Study them carefully and see how each new scale gains an extra flat until eventually we reach the scale of C♭ Major in which every note is flattened.

Each scale is shown here in two halves. This will help you to see how the first half of one scale forms the second half of the scale below it.

Major scales with flats

C	D	E	F		G	A	B	C				
F	G	A	B♭		C	D	E	F		F	Major	1 flat
B♭	C	D	E♭		F	G	A	B♭		B♭	,,	2 flats
E♭	F	G	A♭		B♭	C	D	E♭		E♭	,,	3 ,,
A♭	B♭	C	D♭		E♭	F	G	A♭		A♭	,,	4 ,,
D♭	E♭	F	G♭		A♭	B♭	C	D♭		D♭	,,	5 ,,
G♭	A♭	B♭	C♭		D♭	E♭	F	G♭		G♭	,,	6 ,,
C♭	D♭	E♭	F♭		G♭	A♭	B♭	C♭		C♭	,,	7 ,,

We have stated above that the scale of B♭ Major has 2 flats, although it contains three flat signs. This is because both the first note and the last note is the *tonic*. So both these flats count as one. The same applies to all the other scales below B♭ Major.

Once a note is flattened, it stays flattened in the later scales.

A. In which major scale does A♭ appear as the sub-dominant (fourth) note?

A♭ Major scale	**4**
D♭ Major scale	**6**
E♭ Major scale	**8**

B. In which *other* scales does A♭ appear?

In all scales above E♭ Major	**5**
In all scales except C Major	**7**
In all scales below E♭ Major	**9**

C. In which scales does A♭ *not* appear?

In all scales below E♭ Major	**1**
In C Major only	**2**
In all scales above E♭ Major	**3**

You chose the wrong answer to questions A and B in the last exercise—and you made exactly the same mistake in each of them. You did not read the lesson carefully enough. Let's go through it again.

From C Major to G Major

In what way is the G Major scale similar to the C Major scale? The *first* four notes of the G Major (G A B C) are the same as the *second* four notes of the C Major.

In what way is the G Major scale different from the C Major scale? The *seventh note* (leading note) of the G Major scale is sharpened.

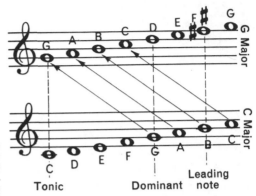

We can now see how to build the G Major scale from the C Major scale. We simply use the *second* four notes of the C Major as the *first* four notes of the new scale—and we sharpen the seventh note of this new scale.

Observe that we are building *upwards*—the first note (tonic) of G Major is four notes above the first note of C Major. Observe too that the seventh note (leading note) of the lower scale becomes the third note of the new scale.

Now tackle the repeat exercise below.

Choose the correct answer in each of these.

A.	What new scale do we get if we build upwards from the C Major scale?	G Major	**2**
		F Major	**6**
		D Major	**7**
B.	How many notes higher is this new scale?	Four notes	**1**
		Three notes	**8**
		One note	**9**
C.	Which note of the new scale must be sharpened?	The note G	**3**
		The note F	**4**
		The note D	**5**

So the harmonic minor scale (page 675) has an 'augmented second'—a leap of 1½ tones—between the sixth and seventh notes: 1 ½ 1 1 ½ <u>1½</u> ½.

The melodic minor scale (ascending)

Melodically speaking, this 1½ tone leap sometimes seems awkward and so early composers were confronted with a problem. The leap had been created because the seventh note of the scale had been sharpened to turn it into a true *leading* note.

So they could not restore this note to a natural note. Only one other solution was left to them—they sharpened the *sixth* note of the scale as well.

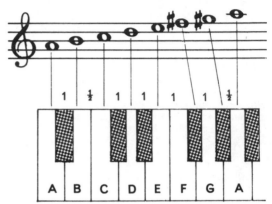

This *reduced* the interval between the sixth note and the seventh note to a *whole* tone. And, at the same time, it *increased* the ½ tone interval between the fifth note and the sixth note to a *whole* tone:

1 ½ 1 1 1 1 ½

This later, more melodic scale is called the *melodic minor scale*.

The melodic minor scale does not have an 'augmented second'.

		1 1 ½ 1 1 1 ½	**3**
A.	The interval pattern of the *major* scale is . . .	1 ½ 1 1 ½ 1½ ½	**4**
		1 ½ 1 1 1 1 ½	**5**
B.	The interval pattern of the *harmonic minor* scale is . . .	1 ½ 1 1 1 1 ½	**1**
		1 1 ½ 1 1 1 ½	**8**
		1 ½ 1 1 ½ 1½ ½	**9**
C.	The interval pattern of the *melodic* minor scale is . . .	1 ½ 1 1 1 1 ½	**2**
		1 ½ 1 1 ½ 1½ ½	**6**
		1 1 ½ 1 1 1 ½	**7**

Almost every piece of music with which we are familiar—long or short, classical or 'pop'—uses the notes of a particular major or minor scale. A piece of music which uses the notes of the D Major scale is said to be in the key of D Major. A piece of music which uses the notes of the A♭ Major scale is said to be in the key of A♭ Major. And so on.

The key signature

When a composer writes in a major key, then—unless he chooses the key of C Major (page 532)—he must show which notes must be sharpened or flattened. If, for example, he writes in the key of G Major (page 937), he must indicate that every F must be *sharpened*. If he writes in the key of F Major (page 196), he must indicate that every B must be flattened.

The composer *could* do this by putting a sharp (or flat) sign before the note concerned every time that note appears. But there is a simpler way. Instead of putting a sharp sign before every G, he puts just *one* sharp sign in the G position *at the beginning of the stave*—just after the clef sign. And he does the same when he wants to indicate that a particular note should be flattened each time it appears. These sharp (or flat) signs directly after the clef sign are called *key signatures*.

Here we have a sharp sign in the F position at the beginning of a piece of music. This means that *every* F must be sharpened.

Here we have a flat sign in the B position at the beginning of a piece of music. This means that *every* B must be flattened.

The key signature makes music simpler to write and read.

B♭	D♭	F♭	**3**
B	D	F	**6**
B♯	D♯	F♯	**9**

A. Name these three notes

B	D	F	**1**
B♯	D♯	F♯	**4**
B	D	F♯	**7**

B. Name these three notes

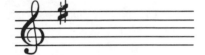

B	D	F	**2**
B♭	D	F	**5**
B♭	D♭	F♭	**8**

C. Name these three notes

Here are the key signatures of the major scales. The only major scale not shown is the C Major scale. This has no sharps or flats—and therefore no signature:

G maj. D maj. A maj. E maj.   B maj.   F♯ maj.   C♯ maj.

F maj. B♭maj. E♭ maj. A♭ maj. D♭ maj.   G♭ maj.   C♭ maj.

So the pattern of tone intervals in the major scale is 1 1 ½ 1 1 1 ½ and we can obtain this pattern by playing the white (natural) notes from C to the C above it. But, if we start on any white note other than C, we can *not* get this pattern—not if we stick to the white notes all the time.

Sharps in the major scale
However, we can get quite close to the major scale pattern if we play all the white (natural) notes from any G to the G above it.

From G to the E above it, the pattern is all right:

1 1 ½ 1 1

All we need now is a whole tone followed by a half tone. But from E to F is only a *half* tone. So, to increase this interval to a whole tone, we must play F *sharp* instead of F:

1 1 ½ 1 1 1

From F sharp to G is a half tone. So we now have the required pattern:

1 1 ½ 1 1 1 ½

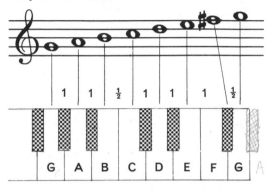

When we raise a natural note by a ½ tone (e.g. from F to F♯) we have *sharpened* it.

Choose the correct answer in each of these.

A.	What is the required pattern of tone intervals in any major scale?	1 1 ½ 1 1 1 ½	**1**
		1 1 1 1 1 1	**2**
		1 1 ½ 1 1 1	**3**
B.	We can obtain this pattern by playing all the white (natural) notes from . . .	any A to the A above it	**5**
		any G to the G above it	**7**
		any C to the C above it	**9**
C.	If we want to play a major scale from G to the G above it, what must we do?	sharpen G	**4**
		sharpen F	**6**
		flatten F	**8**

Correct. You have now completed this course.

The word *major* means 'greater'. The word *minor* means 'smaller'. Why is the major scale 'greater' than the minor scale? It is called *major* because its first three notes—a *major third*—cover two whole tones, whereas the first three notes of a minor scale—a *minor third*—cover only one-and-a-half tones. At the back of this book you will find a complete list of both major and minor scales.

At the back you will also find a subject index. So you may now use this book for reference whenever you wish.

If you would like to check your own performance on this course, here is a simple way to do it.

Look at the record sheet on which you have written down all your attempted three-figure solutions. If you completed the course in only 24 attempts, give yourself full marks. If you look more than 24 attempts, then deduct 5 marks for each extra attempt. Like this:

Number of attempts	Percentage marks	Grading letter
24	100%	A
25	95%	A
26	90%	A
27	85%	A
28	80%	B
29	75%	B
30	70%	B
31	65%	B
32	60%	C
33	55%	C
34	50%	C
35	45%	C
36	40%	D
37	35%	D
38	30%	D
39	25%	D
40	20%	E
41	15%	E
42	10%	E
43	5%	E
44 (or more)	0%	F

Correct. Now read on.

So a major scale that starts on C is in the key of C Major. A major scale that starts on G is in the key of G Major. And so on. Let us compare the G Major scale (page 937) with the C Major scale (page 532).

From C Major to G Major

In what way is the G Major scale similar to the C Major scale? The *first* four notes of the G Major (G A B C) are the same as the *second* four notes of the C Major.

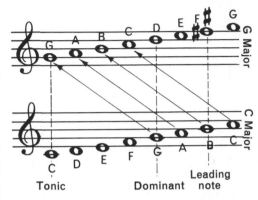

In what way is the G Major scale different from the C Major scale? The *seventh note* (leading note) of the G Major scale is sharpened.

We can now see how to build the G Major scale from the C Major scale. We simply use the *second* four notes of the C Major as the *first* four notes of the new scale—and we sharpen the seventh note of this new scale.

Observe that we are building *upwards*—the first note (tonic) of G Major is four notes above the first note of C Major. Observe too that the seventh note (leading note) of the lower scale becomes the third note of the new scale.

Choose the correct answer in each of these.

A.	What new scale do we get if we build upwards from the C Major scale?	G Major	**2**
		F Major	**6**
		D Major	**7**

B.	How many notes higher is this new scale?	Four notes	**1**
		Three notes	**8**
		One note	**9**

C.	Which note of the new scale must be sharpened?	The note G	**3**
		The note F	**4**
		The note D	**5**

Before going any further, we must take a quick look at the way in which music is written down. This subject is covered in some detail in 'From Notes to Rhythm', the first book in this music series.

The stave

Music is written down on a *stave* (or staff). This is simply a group of five parallel lines. Note symbols are placed on these lines and between these lines.

The higher the pitch of the note, the higher its position on the stave. So, if note A appears *between* the second and third lines of a stave, then note B should appear *on* the third line, just above note A. Note C will then appear *between* the third and fourth lines, just above note B. And so on.

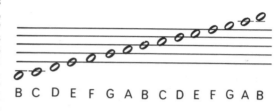

B C D E F G A B C D E F G A B

Ledger lines

A stave can accommodate eleven different pitches of note in all—one note just below the bottom line, one note just above the top line, five notes actually on the lines, and four notes between the lines.

If we want to add any more notes—higher in pitch or lower in pitch—we add short lines above or below the stave. These extra lines are called *ledger lines*.

The higher the note, the higher its position on the stave.

A.	How many notes of different pitch can be placed *on* the lines of any one stave?	four	**1**
		seven	**2**
		five	**3**
B.	How many notes of different pitch can be placed *between* the lines of any one stave?	six	**4**
		five	**6**
		four	**8**
C.	How many notes of different pitch can be accommodated altogether on any one stave?	fifteen	**5**
		thirteen	**7**
		eleven	**9**

WHY NOT 12 MAJOR SCALES?

See page 681

A, (A sharp), B flat, (C flat = B), C, C sharp = D flat, D,

(D sharp =) E flat, (Fb = E), (E# = F), F sharp = G flat, G,

(G sharp =) A flat,

= ~~###~~ possible Major Scales?
21

But only 15.

NO A SHARP B SHARP
D SHARP

A, ... , B flat, (B, = C flat), C, C sharp, = D flat, D,
E flat, E, F, (F sharp, = G flat), G, A flat

MINOR ~~KEYS~~ KEYS INCLUDE Gsharp(= A flat), Dsharp (= E flat) Asharp=Bf
Scales are only used where all flat / all sharp
in key signature?

With variable pitch keyboards, surely
Key signatures ~~scales~~ are irrelevant?
Is scale determined solely by pitch?
      Key signature
The how do composers determine
      How would music be represented?

Hertz? eg starting note 420 Hertz?

WHY IS 'B' CALLED 'C FLAT'
BUT 'E' IS NEVER 'F FLAT'
      F double sharp = G   G double sharp = A.
      C double sharp = D

Major Scales (ascending only).

The C Major scale, from which these scales derive, can be found on page 532
The scales are shown here without key signatures. These key signatures
appear on page 893 (facing).

Major Scales with sharps:

Major Scales with flats:

★ = the newly sharpened note   ★ = the newly flattened note

Harmonic Minor Scales (key signatures with sharps).

The A Minor scale (harmonic) from which these scales derive, can be found on page 675.

Note that, from G♯ Minor onwards, the leading note (already a sharp) is sharpened again to become a double sharp (x). Note also that the keys of D♯ Minor and A♯ Minor are rarely used.

Key E minor. Leading-note, D♯ .

Key B minor. Leading-note, A♯ .

Key F♯ minor. Leading-note, E♯ .

Key C♯ minor. Leading-note, B♯

Key G♯ minor. Leading-note Fx.

Key D♯ minor. Leading-note Cx.

Key A♯ minor. Leading-note, Gx.

+ A minor.

Harmonic Minor Scales (key signatures with flats).

The A Minor scale (harmonic), from which these scales derive, can be found on page 675.

Note that, from C Minor onwards, the leading note (previously a sharp) is flattened and therefore becomes a natural.

Key D minor. Leading-note, C♯.

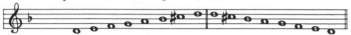

Key G minor. Leading-note, F♯

Key C minor. Leading-note, B♮.

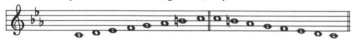

Key F minor. Leading-note, E♮.

Key B♭ minor. Leading-note, A♮.

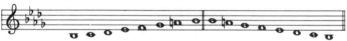

Key E♭ minor. Leading-note, D♮.

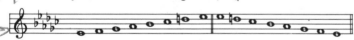

Key A♭ minor. Leading-note, G♮.

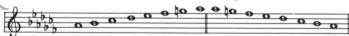

No D flat minor
G flat minor
C flat minor

Melodic Minor Scales (key signatures with sharps).

The A Minor scale (melodic), from which these scales derive, can be found on page 392.

Note that, from G♯ Minor onwards, the leading-note (already a sharp) is sharpened again to become a double-sharp (x). To counterbalance this, the 7th note of the descending scale (previously a natural) now becomes a sharp. Similarly, in A♯ Minor, the 6th note of the descending scale becomes a sharp to counterbalance the sharpening of the 6th note of the ascending scale (now a double-sharp).

Key E minor. Leading-note, D♯

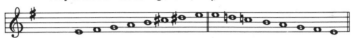

Key B minor. Leading-note, A♯

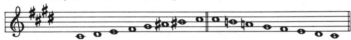

Key F♯ minor. Leading-note, E♯

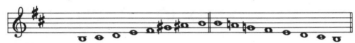

Key C♯ minor Leading-note, B♯

Key G♯ minor. Leading-note, Fx.   *F double sharp (= G)*

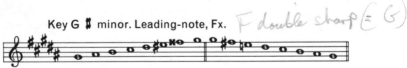

Key D♯ minor. Leading-note, Cx.   *C double sharp (= D)*

Key A♯ minor. Leading-note, Gx.   *G double sharp (= A)*

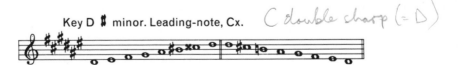

Melodic Minor Scales (key signatures with flats).

The A Minor scale (melodic), from which these scales derive, can be found on page 392. It will be remembered that the 6th and 7th notes of the ascending A Minor scale are both sharps and that the 7th and 6th notes of the descending scale are both naturals.

Note that, from D Minor onwards, the 6th note of the ascending scale (a sharp in the A Minor scale) is flattened to become a natural. To counterbalance this, the 6th note of the descending scale (a natural in the A Minor scale) is flattened to become a flat. And, from C Minor onwards, the same thing happens with the 7th or leading note.

Key D minor. Leading-note, C ♯.

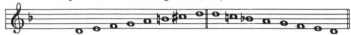

Key G minor. Leading-note, F ♯.

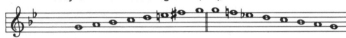

Key C minor. Leading-note, B ♮.

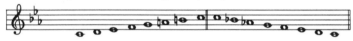

Key F minor. Leading-note, E ♮.

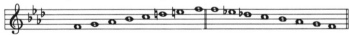

Key B ♭ minor. Leading-note, A ♮.

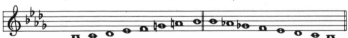

Key E ♭ minor. Leading-note, D ♮.

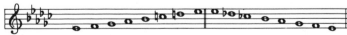

Key A ♭ minor. Leading-note, G ♮.

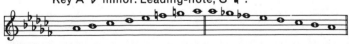

Index